Let's Learn About
MEXICO
ACTIVITY & COLORING BOOK

Yuko Green

DOVER PUBLICATIONS, INC.
Mineola, New York

NOTE

Did you know that Mexican children celebrate their birthdays with parties called *fiestas,* or that most Mexican people (even grown-ups!) take a nap in the middle of the day called a *siesta?*

Inside this exciting and educational coloring and activity book, you can learn all about the country of Mexico while completing mazes, word searches, find-the-differences, and other fun activities. Find out what Mexican money is called, how to count to ten in Spanish, how to make your own *piñata,* and much more.

Copyright
Copyright © 2013 by Yuko Green
All rights reserved.

Bibliographical Note
Let's Learn About MEXICO Activity and Coloring Book is a new work, first published by Dover Publications, Inc., in 2013.

International Standard Book Number
ISBN-13: 978-0-486-48994-0
ISBN-10: 0-486-48994-9

Manufactured in the United States by Courier Corporation
48994901
www.doverpublications.com

HOLA!

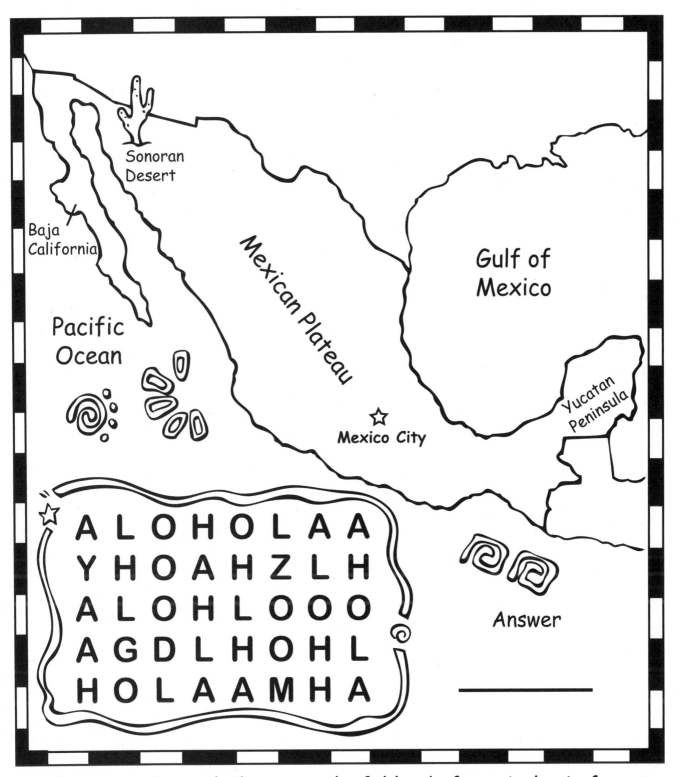

A L O H O L A A
Y H O A H Z L H
A L O H L O O O
A G D L H O H L
H O L A A M H A

Answer

_____

Welcome to Mexico! This is a colorful land of tropical rain forests, volcanoes, deserts, and beaches. You will be greeted by the Spanish word for hello: "Hola (OH-lah)!" How many times can you find **Hola** in the puzzle box? Write your answer in the space provided.

MEXICAN

Many people of Mexico today are of both native Indian and Spanish ancestry. They make up the majority of the Mexican population today. What are they called? To find out, write the first letter of each picture in the box next to it and read the word you have spelled.

PRICKLY HOME

The northern part of the Mexican Plateau is a desert covered with rocks and sand. Connect the dots to see a plant in which many animals make their home. More than 120 species of this plant grow here.

PIÑATA MATCH

People celebrate holidays in Mexico with big fiestas (parties). At many fiestas, children play the piñata game, where blindfolded children use a stick to try and break a decorated container with treats inside. Find and circle the two piñatas that look exactly the same.

SPEAK SPANISH

1. Thank you.   2. Hello.   3. Good-bye.
4. friend (male)   5. friend (female)

Mexico is the world's largest Spanish-speaking country. Write the correct number of the meanings for each Spanish word on the lines provided. Use the pictures as clues.

Code key:

- ♡ = A
- ☽ = C
- ♥ = E
- △ = I
- ○ = J
- ▲ = M
- □ = N
- ★ = O
- ● = T
- ✳ = U
- @ = X
- ☆ = Y

MEXICO

Mexico

Hola from Mexico's capital,

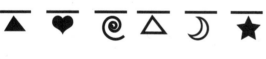

▲ ♥ @ △ ☽ ★
☽ △ ● ☆

Hi from Mexico's major tourist center on the US-Mexico border,

● △ ○ ✳ ♡ □ ♡

Use the code to find out where the postcards are from.

MEXICAN FACTS
Word Search

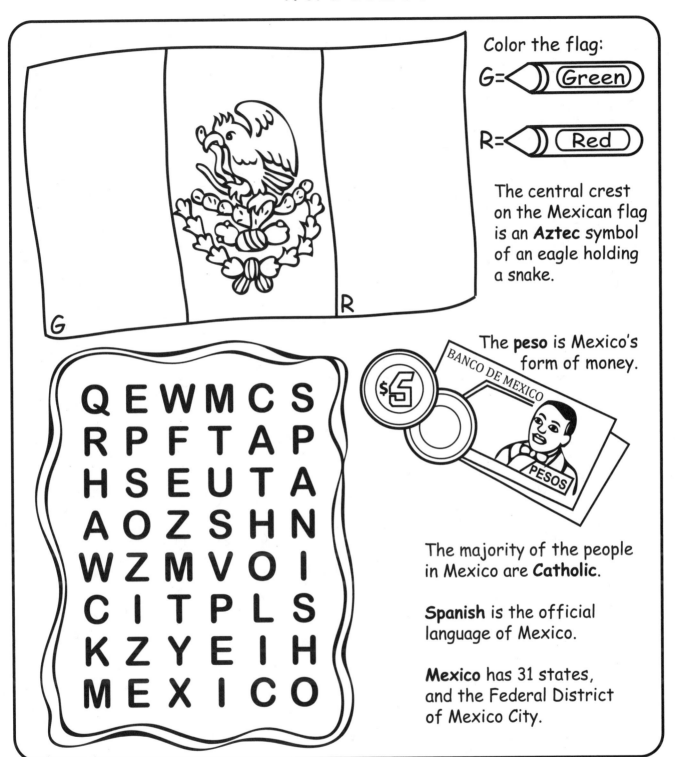

Color the flag:

G= (Green)

R= (Red)

The central crest on the Mexican flag is an **Aztec** symbol of an eagle holding a snake.

The **peso** is Mexico's form of money.

BANCO DE MEXICO

PESOS

The majority of the people in Mexico are **Catholic**.

Spanish is the official language of Mexico.

Mexico has 31 states, and the Federal District of Mexico City.

Q	E	W	M	C	S
R	P	F	T	A	P
H	S	E	U	T	A
A	O	Z	S	H	N
W	Z	M	V	O	I
C	I	T	P	L	S
K	Z	Y	E	I	H
M	E	X	I	C	O

In the puzzle above, find and circle the 5 bold words from the facts listed. Look down, across and diagonal.

MAYA GLYPHS

The Mayans (ancient Mexicans), used special symbols called glyphs as numbers. The numbers 1 through 19 were written using only dots and bars.

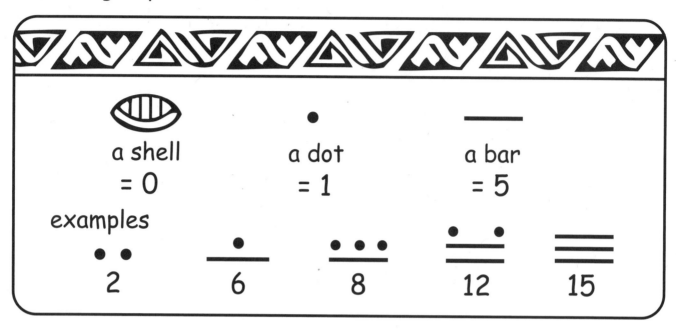

a shell = 0   a dot = 1   a bar = 5

examples

2   6   8   12   15

See if you can use the examples in the box above to help you figure out the numbers for each glyph below.

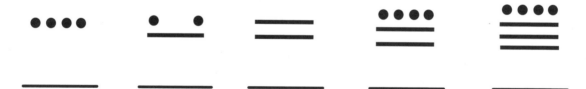

_____   _____   _____   _____   _____

Now solve these arithmetic problems.

$\bullet$ ___ $\bullet$ + $\bullet\bullet\bullet$ = <u> 10 </u>

(bar with two dots above and bar below) + (bar with dot above) = _____

(bar with two dots above and two bars below) − $\bullet\bullet\bullet\bullet$ = _____

NUMBER MATCH-UPS
Mexican Crafts

1 uno (OO-noh)

2 dos (dohs)

3 tres (trace)

4 cuatro (KWAH-troh)

5 cinco (SINK-oh)

Count each group of Mexican crafts and draw a line to the matching number. Learn how to say 1-5 in Spanish too.

TOMATO SCRAMBLE

chetkup

_ _ _ _ _ _ _

zzapi

_ _ _ _ _

spaghetti
ausce

_ _ _ _ _

slaas

_ _ _ _ _

Originating in South America, the tomato was a main staple in Aztec and mayan culture. Tomatoes are still important in Mexican meals. All of the foods above use tomatoes. Unscramble the letters to find out what they are.

JUNGLE ANIMALS

jaguar

opossum

porcupine

alligator

armadillo

```
      o g k g d l j
p o r c u p i n e h a
j l j h o v o c p e g
m y b d o u l s p x u
a c q d o a o j s y a
o l l i d a m r a u r
a l l i g a t o r a m
```

The southern parts of Mexico (the wetter and hotter areas near
the Gulf of Mexico) are tropical rain forests. Find and circle 5
names of jungle animals in the puzzle box. Look down, across,
backward, and diagonally.

CHOCOLATE

cat
_____

_____

_____

_____

_____

_____

_____

_____

Chocolate originally came from Mexico. Hot chocolate was a special drink for the Aztec king. How many words can you make using the letters in the word **chocolate**?

BURRO MAZE

START

END

Mexicans have used burros (small donkeys) for farming and for trips over rough land. The sturdy burro can pull farm wagons and carry loads. Help this boy and his burro go over the mountain trails to get to the town.

NUMBER MATCH-UPS
Mexican Crops

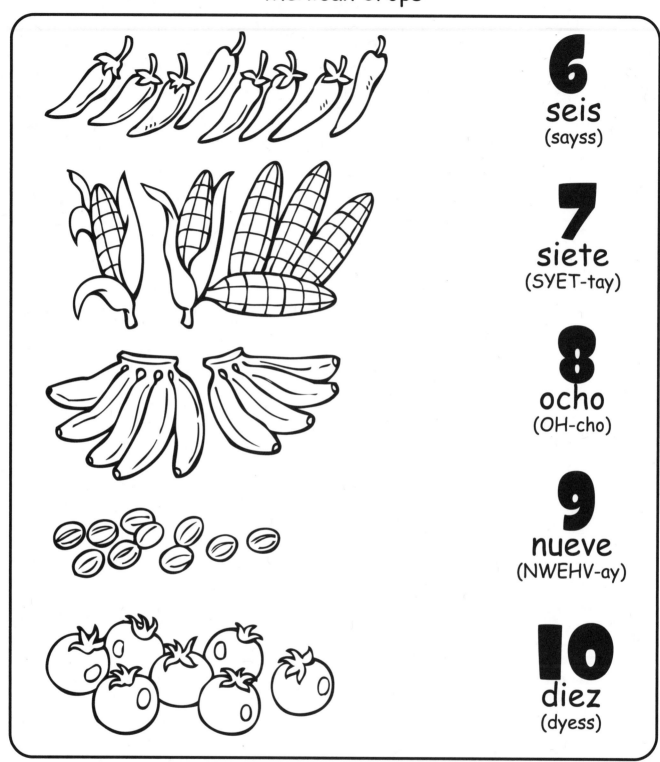

6
seis
(sayss)

7
siete
(SYET-tay)

8
ocho
(OH-cho)

9
nueve
(NWEHV-ay)

10
diez
(dyess)

Many Mexican Indians are farmers. Count each group of crops and draw a line to the matching number. Learn how to say 6–10 in Spanish too.

OH SIESTA

A siesta is a short rest or nap taken in the early afternoon, often after comida (koh-MEE-dah)—the midday meal around 2 o'clock. Find and circle the letters **SIESTA** hidden in the picture above.

MARIACHI MUSIC

The **mariachi** (mah-ree-AH-chee) band is a symbol of Mexico. The groups play at weddings, in parties, squares, and streets.

Find and circle 10 things on this page that make it different from the one on the left.

MADE IN MEXICO

chili

vanilla

poinsettia

tortilla

gum

chihuahua

In addition to chocolate, many other things have a Mexican origin. Fill in the puzzle with the 6 names of the things pictured that come from Mexico.

SAGUARO

Growing in the Sonoran Desert, the **saguaro** (suh-WAH-roe/suh-WAR-oh) provides shelter, food, and moisture for animals. Help each of the four animals find the suguaro cactus in the center.

AZTECS

Aztec pyramid

A   C   E   G   H   I   M   X

___ ___ ___ ___ ___ ___

Aztec Indians in central Mexico had a powerful empire until it was taken over by the Spanish. The Aztecs were great builders and strong warriors. Use the code to fill in the blanks and find out what the Aztecs were originally called.

CELEBRATION!

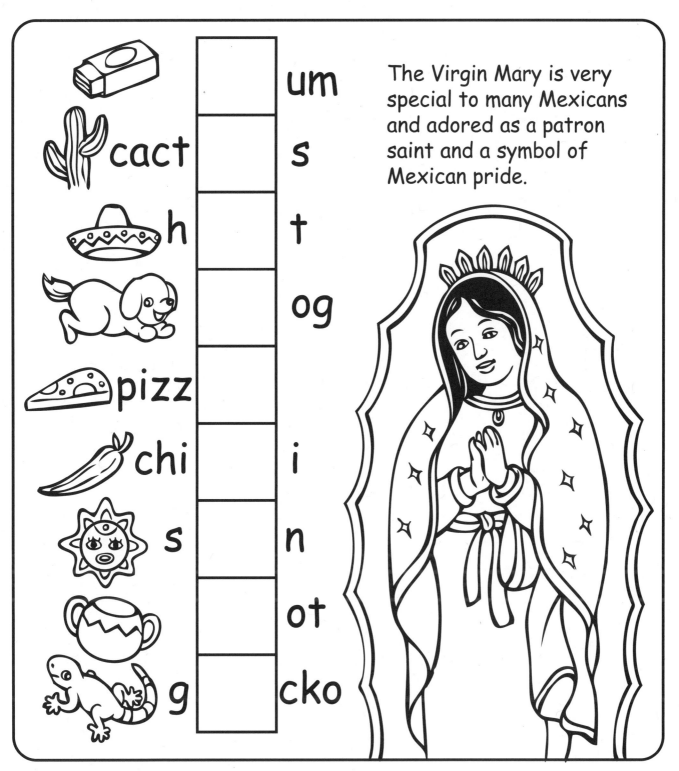

cact **um**

cact **s**

h **t**

og

pizz **i**

chi **n**

s **ot**

g **cko**

The Virgin Mary is very special to many Mexicans and adored as a patron saint and a symbol of Mexican pride.

_____ Day, December 12, is Mexico's most important religious holiday, during which the Virgin Mary is honored. To find out the name of this celebration, fill in the missing letter to spell the name of each picture, then read the word you made from top to bottom.

SMILING SUN

The Aztecs honored the sun and it has long been a popular motif in Mexican arts and crafts. Find and circle the one sun that does not have a match.

WEAVINGS

backstrap loom

skirt
belt
wall-hanging
poncho
blanket
shirt

Women and girls in Mexico make colorful weavings for clothes and for house items. Each Indian village uses its own unique colors and patterns. Fill in the puzzle with the 6 words appearing inside the poncho.

CINCO DE MAYO
Handmade Maracas

What you need:
2 toilet paper rolls
2 handfuls of dried beans (or rice or unpopped popcorn)
aluminum foil (about 8" in length)
4 colored rubber bands
paint (red, green, white)
accessories (feathers, stickers or any decorative items)

1.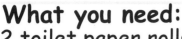
Paint a toilet paper roll.

2.
Cut out 3" x 3" squares from aluminum foil. You need 8 sheets for 2 maracas.

3.
Cover up one end of the roll with two sheets of square foil and secure them with a rubber band.

4.
Add a handful of beans into the roll.

5. Cover up other end of roll with foil and rubber band. Decorate your maraca with feathers, stickers and anything colorful.

Now it's time to make noise!

Cinco de Mayo (5th of May) is a holiday which celebrates the victory of the Mexican army against the French forces in the battle of 1862. The holiday is a symbol of Mexican pride and great festivity with parades, dancing, and food. Join the fun by making a pair of handmade maracas (rattles)!

CORN & BEANS
Word Search

beans

enchiladas

e	n	c	h	i	l	a	d	a	s
t	o	r	t	i	l	l	a	s	n
r	c	c	v	b	g	b	o	t	a
u	w	h	o	q	e	h	i	l	c
t	a	c	o	r	t	a	l	n	h
x	h	g	z	h	n	f	n	n	o
k	b	u	r	r	i	t	o	s	j

burritos

corn

nacho

nacho

tortillas

taco

The staples of Mexican diet are typically corn and beans. A tortilla is flat bread made from corn and is used in many Mexican foods. A variety of beans are used in daily Mexican food. Find the seven names of Mexican foods in the puzzle above.

SPORTS IN MEXICO

futbol

rodeo

i

baseball

bullfighting

boxing

rodeo

Mexico's favorite sports are futbol (soccer) and baseball. Boxing and bullfighting are popular too. Mexico's national sport is rodeo. Finish the puzzle above with these names of Mexican sports.

CHARROS

Mexican cowboys are called charros. Find and circle 11 things in the top picture that make it different from the one on the bottom.

BUTTERFLY MAZE

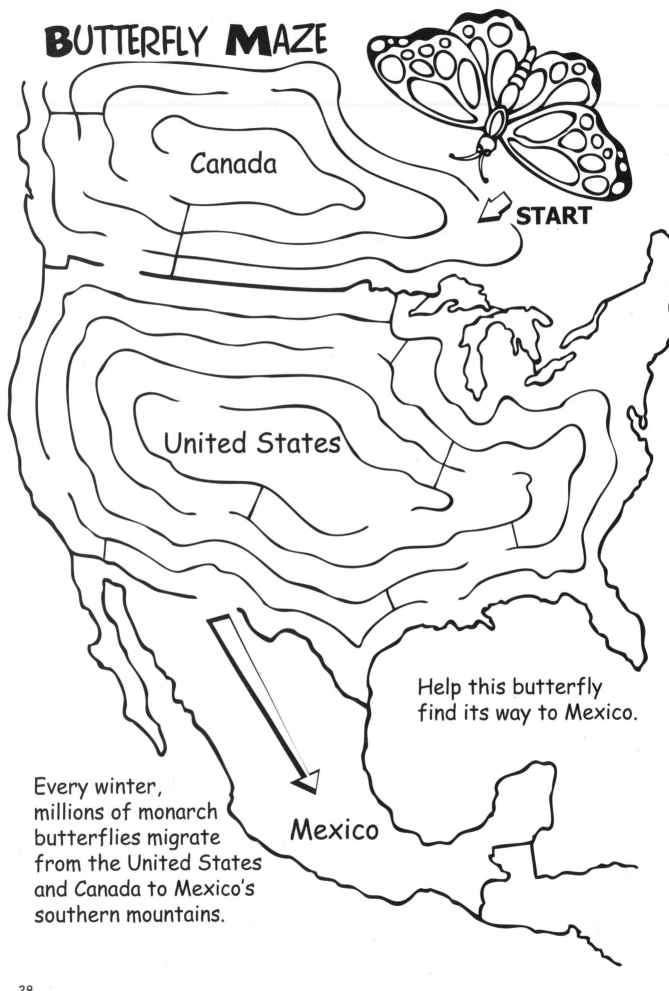

START

Canada

United States

Help this butterfly find its way to Mexico.

Mexico

Every winter, millions of monarch butterflies migrate from the United States and Canada to Mexico's southern mountains.

READY TO DANCE?

Mexico has a long tradition of dance that expresses its rich and colorful heritage. Mexican folk dances have varied forms in style, from those originated in the ancient cultures of Aztec and Maya, to the ones influenced by Spanish and other European dances.

GENTLE GIANT

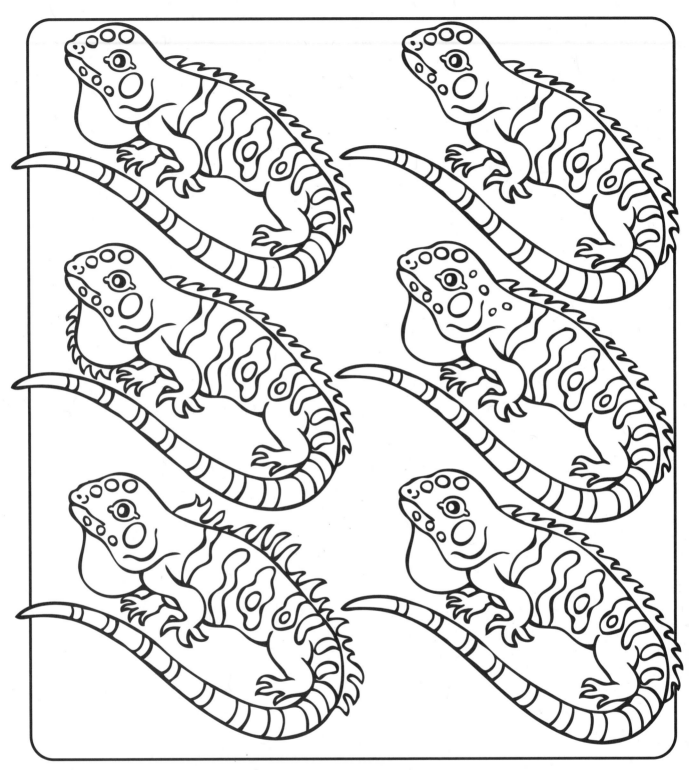

The green iguana lives in the jungle of Southern Mexico. This giant lizard looks fierce, but it is actually very timid. It uses its sharp claws to climb up branches to the jungle canopy. Find and circle the two iguanas that look exactly alike.

DAY OF

THE DEAD

🌀 = A
❀ = D
✿ = E
☆ = F
♥ = H
✤ = O
⊛ = T
♡ = Y

This is a vibrant and fun festival (October 31 to November 2) in Mexico, which celebrates and honors the memory of those who have passed. There are many colorful decorations, including brightly colored sugar skulls, skeletons, and masks. Use the code to find out the name of this joyous festival.

LETTER FROM MEXICO

Hola!

My name is Selena. I live in Mexico.
I live on a **farm**, just like many of my friends.
My cousins live in a small **village** near by.

My family has goats, cows and
chickens for meat, milk and eggs.
I help take care of them with
my 2 brothers and 3 sisters.

our family
burro

Last summer I visited my friend in
Mexico City. It was a super big **city**
and we had lots of fun!

What kind of clothes do you wear in your
country? In Mexico, many boys and men wear white
cotton t-shirts, pants, and leather **sandals**, called
huaraches. To protect them from our
hot sun and rain,
they wear wide-brimmed
hats called **sombreros**. I usually
wear cotton **skirts** and **blouses**. My
mom adds pretty embroidery on my blouses.
Adios!

Selena

n o t t o c s c w
b s o m b r e r o
l l v h z w h s l
e n o i a x c k a
a h g u l t a i d
t w s n s l r r n
h m r a f e a t a
e c i t y s u g s
r b q p i h h c e

After you read the letter on the left page, complete these two activities.

Word Search

Find all 10 bold words from the letter in the puzzle. Look up, down, across, and diagonally.

Friend Maze

Help Selena visit her friend in Mexico City.

START

END

DESERT LIFE

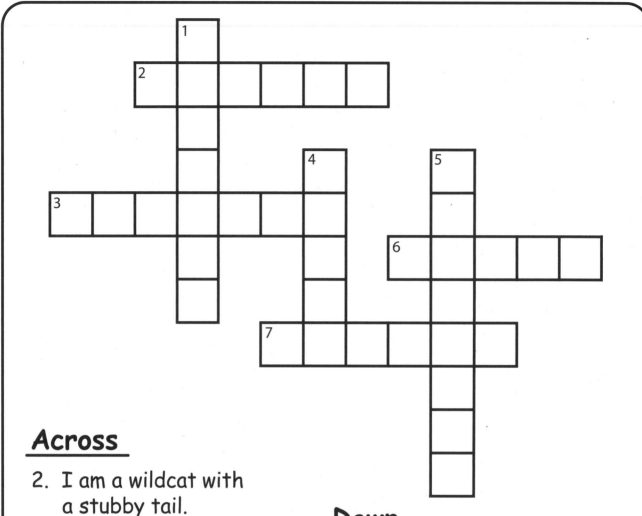

Across

2. I am a wildcat with a stubby tail.
3. I look for bodies of dead animals from the sky.
6. I am small, skinny and long with red, yellow, and black bands.
7. I am a wild dog and often howl at the moon.

Down

1. I am the poisonous lizard with a colorful body.
4. I am the lizard with yellow-and-brown bands .
5. I have a long tail with rings and am a member of the raccoon family.

Deep canyons and rocky deserts cover much of northern Mexico's Sonoran Desert. Fill in the puzzle with 7 wild animals that live in this area. Use the pictures on the right page as clues.

turkey **vulture**

bobcat

coyote

coral **snake**

ringtail

banded **gecko**

gila **monster**

COLORFUL MEXICO

a	n	a	r	a	j	a	d	o	v
a	m	a	r	i	l	l	o	r	i
r	q	j	v	a	z	u	l	o	o
t	s	i	y	e	r	z	x	j	l
z	l	r	z	u	r	o	d	o	e
b	l	a	n	c	o	d	s	i	t
s	u	a	c	n	o	o	e	a	a

anarajado
(orange)

verde
(green)

blanco
(white)

rojo
(red)

amarillo
(yellow)

azul
(blue)

rosa
(pink)

violeta
(violet)

Mexican artists are known for their colorful crafts. Find the bold
Spanish words on each paint pail in the puzzle box above. Look
down, across and diagonally.

rojo (ROH-hoh), anarajado (ah-nar-an-HAH-tho), amarillo (ah-mah-REE-yoh), verde (BEAR-day),
azul (ah-SOOL), rosa (ROH-sah), violeta (vee-oh-LEH-tah), blanco (BLAHN-koh)

PARTY TIME
Making a Piñata

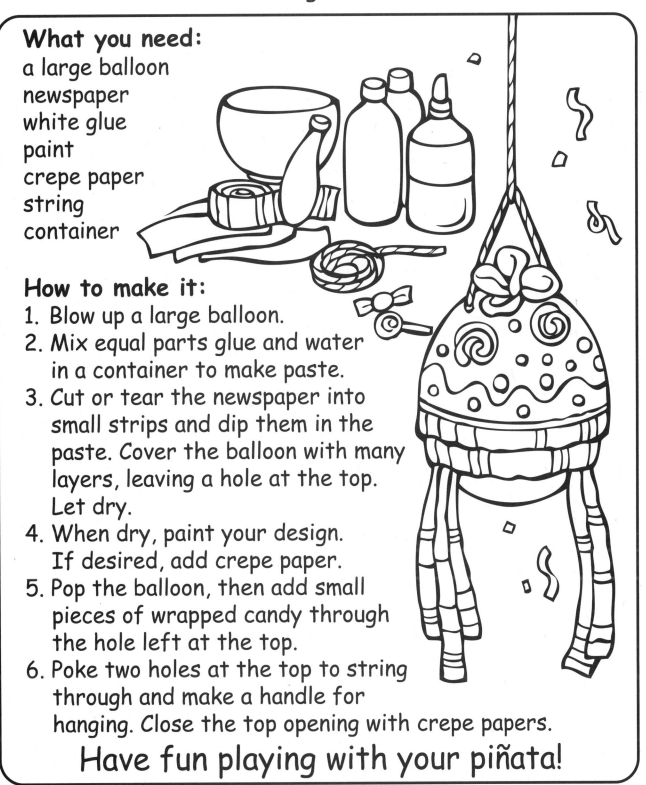

What you need:
a large balloon
newspaper
white glue
paint
crepe paper
string
container

How to make it:
1. Blow up a large balloon.
2. Mix equal parts glue and water in a container to make paste.
3. Cut or tear the newspaper into small strips and dip them in the paste. Cover the balloon with many layers, leaving a hole at the top. Let dry.
4. When dry, paint your design. If desired, add crepe paper.
5. Pop the balloon, then add small pieces of wrapped candy through the hole left at the top.
6. Poke two holes at the top to string through and make a handle for hanging. Close the top opening with crepe papers.

Have fun playing with your piñata!

The piñata was traditionally made of paper mache and shaped like a star. Today they are in all types of shapes, including animals and flowers. Make your own piñata for your next party!

PARTY TIME
Designing a Piñata and Poncho

Decorate the piñata and the boy's poncho
any way you like. Look through this activity book for design ideas.

PAPEL PICADO

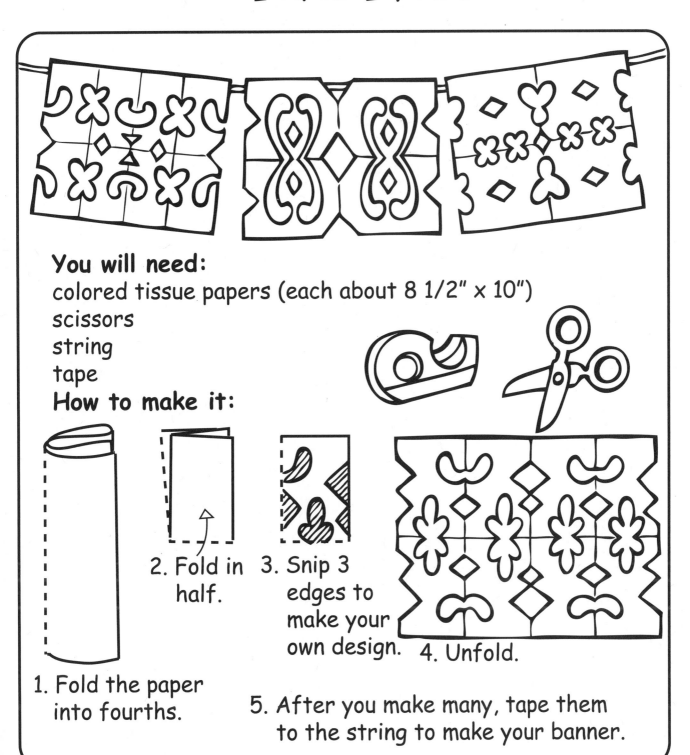

You will need:
colored tissue papers (each about 8 1/2" x 10")
scissors
string
tape

How to make it:

1. Fold the paper into fourths.

2. Fold in half.

3. Snip 3 edges to make your own design.

4. Unfold.

5. After you make many, tape them to the string to make your banner.

Paper (papel) picado is a traditional craft in Mexico. The people create paper picado banners of colorful tissue paper to use as decorations to celebrate holidays and festive occasions. The process is like making a paper snowflake.

SOLUTIONS

HOLA!

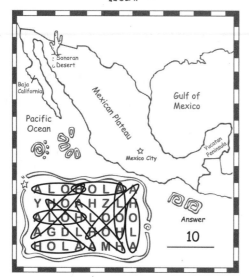

page 1

MEXICAN

page 2

PRICKLY HOME

page 3

PIÑATA MATCH

page 4

SPEAK SPANISH

1. Thank you.   2. Hello.   3. Good-bye.
4. friend (male)   5. friend (female)

page 5

POSTCARDS FROM MEXICO

♡ = A
☾ = C
♥ = E
△ = I
○ = J
▲ = M
□ = N
★ = O
● = T
✿ = U
☆ = Y

Hola from Mexico's capital,

M E X I C O
▲ ♥ ☆ △ ☾ ★

C I T Y
☾ △ ● ☆

Hi from Mexico's major tourist center on the US-Mexico border,

T I J U A N A
● △ ✿ ✿ ♡ □ ♡

Use the code to find out where the postcards are from.

page 6

MEXICAN FACTS
Word Search

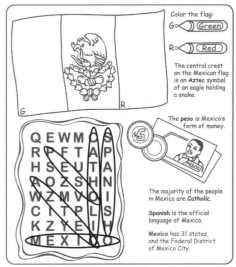

Color the flag:
G = Green
R = Red

The central crest on the Mexican flag is an **Aztec** symbol of an eagle holding a snake.

The **peso** is Mexico's form of money.

The majority of the people in Mexico are **Catholic**.

Spanish is the official language of Mexico.

Mexico has 31 states, and the Federal District of Mexico City.

```
Q E W M O S
R D F T A P
H S E U T A
A O Z S H N
W Z M V O I
C I T P L S
K Z Y E I H
M E X I C O
```

page 7

MAYA GLYPHS

The Mayans (ancient Mexicans), used special symbols called glyphs as numbers. The numbers 1 through 19 were written using only dots and bars.

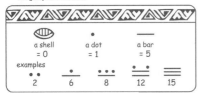

a shell = 0   a dot = 1   a bar = 5

examples
2   6   8   12   15

See if you can use the examples in the box above to help you figure out the numbers for each glyph below.

4   7   10   14   19

Now write your answers to these arithmetic problems.

examples

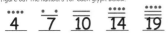 + ••• = 10

•• + • = 18

•• - •••• = 13

page 8

NUMBER MATCH-UPS
Mexican Crafts

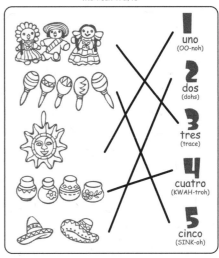

1 uno (OO-noh)
2 dos (dohs)
3 tres (trace)
4 cuatro (KWAH-troh)
5 cinco (SINK-oh)

page 9

TOMATO SCRAMBLE

chetkup
k e t c h u p

zzapi
p i z z a

spaghetti sausce
s a u c e

slaas
s a l s a

page 10

41

JUNGLE ANIMALS

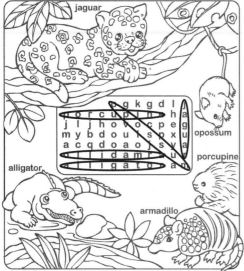

jaguar

opossum

porcupine

alligator

armadillo

```
g k g d l h
p o r c u p i n e h e
j l j h o b o c p e x
m y b d o u t s p s u
a c q d o a o d s y a
l i d a m u l l n r
a l l i g a t o r a n
```

page 11

CHOCOLATE

cat

at
chat
cloth
coach
coat
cocoa
cool
each
eat, hat, hot,
late, taco,
tea, toe...

page 12

BURRO MAZE

START

END

page 13

NUMBER MATCH-UPS
Mexican Crops

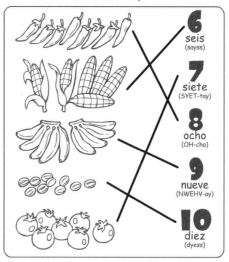

6 seis (sayss)

7 siete (SYET-tay)

8 ocho (OH-cho)

9 nueve (NWEHV-ay)

10 diez (dyess)

page 14

OH SIESTA

page 15

42

page 17

MADE IN MEXICO

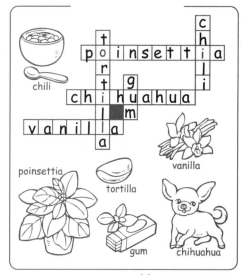

page 18

SAGUARO

page 19

AZTEC

page 20

CELEBRATION!

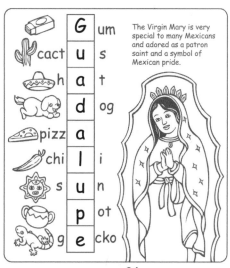

G um
cact u s
h a t
d og
pizz a
chi l i
s u n
p ot
g e cko

The Virgin Mary is very special to many Mexicans and adored as a patron saint and a symbol of Mexican pride.

page 21

SMILING SUN

page 22

WEAVINGS

backstrap loom

skirt
belt
wall-hanging
poncho
blanket
shirt

page 23

CORN & BEANS
Word Search

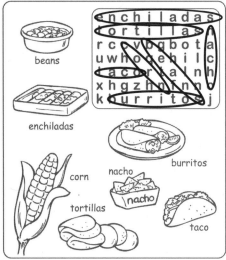

beans

enchiladas

corn

nacho

tortillas

burritos

taco

page 25.

SPORTS IN MEXICO

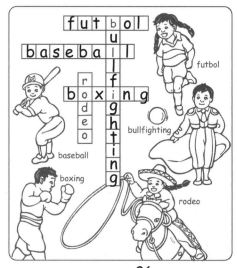

futbol

baseball

bullfighting

boxing

rodeo

page 26

CHARROS

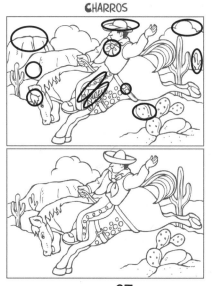

page 27

44

BUTTERFLY MAZE

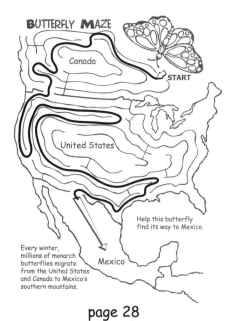

Canada

United States

START

Help this butterfly find its way to Mexico.

Every winter, millions of monarch butterflies migrate from the United States and Canada to Mexico's southern mountains.

Mexico

page 28

GENTLE GIANT

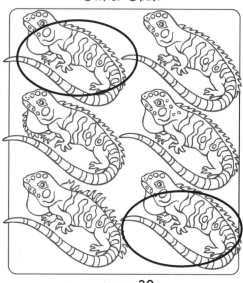

page 30

HAPPY HOLIDAY

D a y   o f

t h e   d e a d

⚘ = A
⚘ = D
⚘ = E
✦ = F
♥ = H
⚘ = O
✪ = T
♡ = Y

page 31

After you read the letter on the left page, complete these two activities.

Word Search
Find all 10 bold words from the letter in the puzzle. Look up, down, across, and diagonally.

Friend Maze
Help Selena visit her friend in Mexico City.

START

END

page 33

DESERT LIFE

m
b o b c a t
o
n
s
v u l t u r e   g   r
t   e   i
e   c   s n a k e
r   k   n
c o y o t e
    g
    t
    a
    i
    l

Across

2. I am a wildcat with a stubby tail.
3. I look for bodies of dead animals from the sky.
6. I am small, skinny and long with red, yellow, and black bands.
7. I am a wild dog and often howl at the moon.

Down

1. I am the poisonous lizard with colorful body.
4. I am the lizard with yellow-and-brown bands.
5. I have a long tail with rings and am number of raccoon family.

page 34

COLORFUL MEXICO

anarajado (orange)

verde (green)

blanco (white)

rojo (red)

amarillo (yellow)

azul (blue)

rosa (pink)

violeta (violet)

page 36